ROUGH GROUND REVISITED

KATE BRAID

CAITLIN PRESS

For my mother, Mary Elizabeth
and in memory of my father, Harry Braid

Thank you

One does not always plant one's feet daintily
when one is covering rough ground.
—Emily Carr, *Journals*

CONTENTS

THE BIRTH OF BUILDINGS

Think Like a Weightlifter, Think Like a Woman

First day on the job and the foreman orders
in a voice like a chainsaw,
Hoist those timbers
by hand to the second floor.
Crane's broken down.

I keep my mouth shut
with difficulty, knowing
how much a six-by-six timber weighs—
twelve feet long and fresh
from the Fraser River.

Lorne, my partner, says nothing,
addresses the modest mountain of timbers
towering over our heads, smelling
sweetly nostalgic for forest.

Weighing in with the wood he faces
with a belly like a great swelling bole,
he shakes off my motion to help and
bends as if to pick up a penny,
scoops up the timber and packs it fifty feet
to lean against the damp grey sides
of the concrete core.
When he doesn't look back,
it's my turn.

And now, because I need this job
and because it's the first day
and because every eye is watching The Girl,
I bend my knees as the book says,
think like a weightlifter, take the beam
by its middle and order my body
to lift.

Reluctantly, the great tree sweating pitch
parts from its peers with a sucking sound
and the beam and I sway to the designated spot.
I drop it. Repeat.

Alone, I carry beams to Lorne
who alone heaves them with the slightest grunt
to the labourer who bends from the second floor
calling *Faster! Faster!*

No, I think. *I will never be a carpenter. Never
able to work like these men.*

Then, Lorne falters.
I see his fatigue.
Without thinking I reach up
and push with all my might.
The beam flies to the second floor and mindless,
I turn to fetch him another.

Without a word
Lorne follows me back to the pile,
lifts one end and helps me
carry the next timber to the wall.
Without a word we both push it up,
continue this path together, find a rhythm,
a pace that feels like dancing.

Lorne says, *You walk different.*
Yes. For I am suddenly
a woman with the strength of two.

CONCRETE FEVER

for Phil Vernon

Seven and one half yards of concrete
and every last pebble in place.
A certain kind of concrete steps
I've never built before and
six different patio slopes that
by the end of this day must run
with perfect symmetry
to one posthole marker of a drainpipe,
with an architect eagle-eye antsy for the least mistake
or merely visual flaw.

I worry, I curse, I adjust and nail
and by six o'clock my steps are a grace
to behold, a joy to walk upon,
and the water from the hose
of the concrete finisher
rolls sweetly down all those six slopes
and into that bull's-eye drain.

I love water!
I love concrete!
I love the work I did today!

Woman's Touch

Lunchtime. We're sitting on a lumber pile
in the middle of a construction site
when my eye falls on Sam's 32-ounce hammer
with the 24-inch handle.

How come all our tools
are longer than they are wide? I ask.

Silence.

Feeling reckless with confidence because
that morning I cut my first set of stairs
at a perfect fit, I push on.

How come the hammer, the saw,
everything except the tool belt looks like
you know what?

Don't be so sensitive, Sam says.
How else could they be?
There's a chorus of grunts in the bass mode.
Besides, (Sam's on firm ground now)
the circular saw is round.

Ed raises his head.
The circular saw was invented by a woman,
he says, and takes a bite of salami.

He finishes the meat, then,
contemplating his Oreo, tells us
that in 1810 in New England,
Sarah Babbitt's husband had a sawmill
where they cut logs over a pit
with a man at each end of a huge handsaw.
One day she noticed
how they wasted half their energy.

Ed doesn't have to tell the carpenters here
that North American handsaws only cut on the push.
He takes a bite of his cookie and chews.
Even Sam is quiet. Ed swallows, carries on.
*She went into her kitchen, fetched a tin dish
and cut teeth in it. Then she slipped it
onto the spindle of her spinning wheel,
fed a cedar shake into it,
and the circular saw was born.*

Ed folds his brown paper bag.
After a certain silence, Sam stands. Spits.
*I knew there was something funny
about that saw,* he says
and sulks off stomping sawdust.

THE PERFECT SETTING FOR PINK

It's a foul morning
when I wake up grumbling about
the ungodly hours of construction,
then drop my Thermos,
condemned to thirst all day
and late to work after cleaning up
the mess.

There's a lecture from the boss,
who sticks me in a ditch
building an afterthought of a wall.
When the hammer slips
I'm covered in muck, curse
the bad judgment that brought me here.

Then sun breaks through
and just for a second, balanced
on the slippery black rubber of my toe,
rests the single petal
of a glorious fuchsia bloom.

RECIPE FOR A SIDEWALK

Pouring concrete is just like baking a cake.
The main difference is,
first you build the pans.
Call them forms. Think grand.

Mix the batter with a few simple ingredients:
> one shovel of sand
>> one shovel of gravel
>>> a pinch of cement.

Add water 'til it's the thickness of cakes.

Can be mixed by hand or with a beater called
a Readi-Mix truck.
Pour into forms and smooth off.
Adjust the heat so it's not too cold,
not too hot. Protect from rain.
Let cook until tomorrow.
Remove the forms and walk on it.

There is one big difference from cakes.
This one will never disappear.
For the rest of your life your kids
will run on the same sidewalk, singing,
My mom baked this!

HANDS

I want to write construction workers' hands—
what they do, how they rip down, build up, how they hurt.
Hands that can't wait, too busy building.

I want to write hands swollen raw
in the rain, in January, carrying
60-pound formply 100 feet in the cold.
Nicks and slivers, tattoos of cedar and fir,
the sting of nails, bite of saw, suck of cement
on fists and fingers fat with muscle.

I want to write small hands like mine,
a woman's hands finding other ways to carry,
smaller pockets when there is a moment
that doesn't call for a hammer or a nail.

I want to write the grace of hands,
men's and women's lifting lumber, sharing the load.
Bring that beam! A foreman's fingers
making exclamation points for a living.

I want to write hands pounding tables,
demanding justice for all, proud
of raising dust, raising walls, high-rises and houses,
construction workers laughing over strong working hands.

One day I will use my hands
to write those hands.

First Date

I put my hands on the café table
right after you notice the hammers
I wear for earrings.
An accidental gesture
      sort of.

I want to show you
the hands that wield a hammer,
so there'll be no illusions
about me
      tough woman
      tough hands.

I don't want you getting the wrong idea
about me
      looking so feminine
      in some parts.
What you see, my hands say for me,
is what you get.

I put my hands on the table,
      tentative
      proud
hoping you're one of the men
who likes a working hand

and scared you're not.

it is the world outside my door which looks at times insane and exceedingly dangerous. it is my own inability that is so dangerous. the worst is that we (that we again) have made it so. no, the worst is, we had no say in how it was made… perhaps that explains why our writing, which we also live inside of, is different from men's, and not a tool, not a "pure instrument for getting a grip on the world."

—Daphne Marlatt, *Ana Historic*

1. Hammer

Hammer, you are number one—androgyne.
Don't tell how I love your shape, long like a man,
the ridges in your sides rubbed smooth
like a woman
by my hand.

Let me hold you close
to the callus
guide your energy
flow of head to nail
to wood
to waler and stud.
All my power to drive
further
into the place
I love
the best
the wood.
Drive it
home
my man
power
woman

power
mine.

Yes!

2. Saw

You're the sensitive one,
unforgiving, impatient
with your own power.

You're never afraid, chant or whine
or growl depending on how I treat you.
Always a talker, those teeth can bite,
rough stuff on wood—or flesh.

I'll take you straight
to the wood, no fooling around.
Eat now—nibble on chamfer,
gobble the garden posts.
You are my Amazon, witch
in the magic of divide and create.

Some call you aggressive but you
are the Zen tool, want a clear hand
to draw you straight to the heart
of fir and cedar and pine.
If I force you, you'll scream.
It takes ears, only ears to know
how this carpenter loves her saw.

3. Nail Puller

Yes, you're lovely, ticklish
with laughter! When my nails are
stuck or "bend in the wind" or
hiding, I smile,
knowing you're close in my belt.

Irresistible, you are
a trick of the hand, tap
of the hammer. Nails
sing with the ease of it,
can't wait to come out, come out
when you call.

4. Tool Belt

Soft pockets, like a mouth
give kisses.
Mother-like, you've built a home
for the family, filling every need
for pencils and nails,
chalk line, hammer and wrench.
Hugging my hips with arms
that adjust to anything,
you're tender and tough,
hold everything
together.

5. Tape Measure

Tough, laying down a hard line of
order: five! six! seven! There's
no fooling around as you pit the force
of your small black fingers
against chaos.

We all stand back for this suck-your-cheeks-in
straight-ahead lady as you roll out numbers
like buns on bake day.
Only a click to your red-shoed feet
can make you pause
in gobbling up all that consequence.

6. Framing Square

You're too stiff for words.
Have *no*
sense of humour.
Ever. Always see things
in perfect proportion.

Here is the voice of reason.
How else
could roofs and angles,
staircases flow from all that
straight-line lumber?

Small arm to large arm,
rise to run. I don't talk
when you're planning
things symmetrical,
methodical, arithmetical,
putting the world
in proportion,
building me castles
in air.

7. Shovel

You're my man
tool rutting
in the garden.
Inquisitor
of the soft dark,
you stand
dripping
in a fine rain
boasting
elbow grease
and sweat.

Before engines
and gasoline
you were
the tough one,
boss man's
biggest muscle.

Your Woodenness
gloats:
plenty here
for a hard hand—
so smooth!
so long!

You'll service any need:
the faster,
the tougher,
the deeper,
the better.
Boast
a cool arm
to lean upon.

Smug as any soldier,
rigid
in fall's garden,
indispensible
for the big, the messy,
the mean…

But today you make no points with me.

All that callus, all those scars
might impress other girls but
in this garden I want small,
I want quiet, want
my very own hand—
held silver.

I'll take the small spade,
thanks. Take my time, slow
over dark earth
let the worms slip aside,
seeds fall.
I'll dig.

"ALWAYS KEEP YOUR TOOLS IN SHAPE"
—Carpenter's manual

I ask my body now,
pump my breasts for information.
Does the skin tingle?
Is my joy aware of itself?
Is there a sort of exuberance
underneath it all, a foundation
of ebb and flow
and does the moontide sing in my veins?

DOOR

doors left ajar.
What else can be said
about a room, its occupants.
———Sue Sinclair, "Doorways"

Saucy thing

  this door invites dance, extends

  brass knuckles.

If you accept, you too
           can swing.

Take hold, terrified

    let go, your

whole body
           forward
                    hair swinging

                        like wild!

This side.

    Now that.

Hinges hold you

        as you fling

   through the whole

half
    circle

so easy

one small step

    to the other side

     where nothing's the same.

On the Roof with Death

When sawdust rolls like marbles under our boots
on the newly sheathed roof three storeys up

we talk of falling. *It's like butter boxes,* Dale says.
We could slide real good. Only hurts when you land!

He yells this suddenly
as if to warn the neighbours.

Dale is a journeyman.
I am his apprentice.

You know the people who live for the moment, he says,
laughing. *They yell "Whee!" all the way down.*

Ph.D.

Lorne is a good carpenter,
catches the foreman's mistakes,
knows what's coming next.
Today when he learns
I have an English degree,
we stop work while he pulls out
the blue bandana stored
like a good-luck token
in his left back pocket.
He rubs the back of his neck,
eyes the wall we're building
and approves.

I'm a professional, he announces.
Built office towers, pulp mills, dams.
Four years apprentice to a carpenter, same
as your bachelor of arts, plus twenty-six more
perfecting my hand. You could say
I have a Ph.D. in construction.

For the rest of the job I call him
Doctor Lorne.

METAMORPHOSIS

Lumber yard. Tool rental. Tarpaulin shop.
These are the clubhouses of the men
where they talk real loud,
flaunt posters of naked women,
bump tattoos.

All morning I pad on kitten's feet
from one to the other, purring
so as not to offend.

But tonight I yearn to ask—
where are the clubhouses of the women?
Where can a carpenter put up her boots,
slam her hardhat to the counter
and roar like a lion in heat?

The Little Poem

Size is a big thing in construction.
Everything is measured and found wanting—
tools, materials, people.

> *How big is your hammer?*
> *Is that all?*
> *Don't you have anything heavier?*
> *Is that the best you can do?*

After a while I wonder,
couldn't we do as well with smaller parts,
more skill?
Imagine building a tower
with teeny-weeny hammers
and a big heart?
There'd be less to throw away
and less to clean.

An itsy-bitsy tower would linger near the ground,
smell the daisies.
Think how far moonlight could travel
over such a delicate space.
We'd cut fewer trees and haul less rock.
Smaller hands, a woman's perhaps,
could build this tower very well.
With less to make, less to borrow, less to buy,
we might spend more time
thinking of little, dreaming dreams
small enough to put our arms around.

New Job: 6 a.m.

The air this morning smells sweet.
A whiff of adrenalin
tightens my knees,
knots my stomach.

Something in my throat
tells me another test's coming
of endurance, of care.

I'm getting ready
to be the exception
again.

It takes time, takes adjustment, takes
tinkering with my thoughts, my attitude,
my withered heart.

After twelve years in the trade,
this is the best it's ever been.

SISTER IN THE BROTHERHOOD

SISTER IN THE UNITED BROTHERHOOD OF CARPENTERS & JOINERS OF AMERICA

I have to take away
the parts of me
that are woman,
have to not care.
It's a skill I learn
from the men's
white granite confidence.
They smile as I leave.
Be tough!
They say it
kindly

> *women can't*
> *take it you have*
> *to be hard*
> *like nails, ha ha*
> *look at me*

The men own the words,
so far.
I learn their language
down cold, hide
behind concrete,
learn to love
that it is soft
and hard at once.

It's not you, **the men say,**
you're much too sensitive
I only said, don't
call me Person
you joined
the Brotherhood we're
in this together
it was mine
first

It doesn't really hurt
if I take apart my
soft self, put my Woman
in a basket
send her away to be
reclaimed
someday
if I'm not lost forever
by then

you can't be pushy
they say, *can't rush*
some things one day
you'll understand
everything
trust me
you won't feel a thing.

ELASTIC BAND
for Alice

We're on the phone and my friend Alice says she's all right. It's
just a little rough right now, just that she's the first woman to teach
mechanics at this school. There was no course before and she
has to make it up as she goes along. *A great opportunity,* the Chief
Instructor told her and agreed to pay her 140 hours prep time
which sounded like a lot only she just found out the usual is five
times that but *Times are tough* the Chief said and Alice should be
grateful for the job. He's never hired a woman before.

Her class is all men, of course, most of them older than she is or
think they are, and several have come because they couldn't get into
any other trade. The counsellor told them small engines are a cinch,
why there's even a woman teacher! And it's true, Alice makes it look
easy. I took a course from her once and she made even the hardest
stuff seem like a breeze. After twenty years' experience and working
everywhere including mines and motorcycle shops and other
schools, she knows her trade deep in her body but here,
the Chief didn't like her from the moment he set eyes on her and
she's not sure what she did wrong but she could sure use a hand,
maybe someone to help her do the marking. The teacher in the next
office has two assistants but times are tough and he needs them
both and Alice is new. The Chief Instructor says she'll figure it out
somehow.

One of her students says she can't fail him because he took
a special math class but Alice says he's expected to remember what
he learned there and he says it's not his fault he can't do fractions.
The Chief Instructor says maybe Alice isn't teaching it right. The
student says he knows better than Alice because he has a friend
who's a machinist who told him different. When Alice shows him
the manual he just looks surprised and says, *Why didn't you say so?*
And when she throws him out of class the Chief Instructor says she
can't do that.

Alice says the pressure is getting to her but it's only another six months until the end of term except the Chief Instructor has told her students they can stick around longer if they need more time and Alice says sometimes she doesn't know how she's going to get through another day. The Chief Instructor says it's sink or swim for her and *Don't forget, we're watching you*. She'll swim of course, she says, she always has, only she's glad she has friends, hopes I don't mind that she called. She just thinks maybe there's a time, is there a time when someone finally says, All right. You've paid your dues. You're in.

She's sorry to bother me, she just wonders if human beings have limits, is it possible we're each given one cup that fills up over the course of our lives, every little test and doubt and question and demand for proof adding one more drop. Is there just so much a body can take, she wonders, do we fill up and overflow? Are we like those elastic bands that break down over time? She just wonders if I ever think of that, just needed to ask.

CONSTRUCTION WORKER'S PRAYER

Our foreman, which art in the First Aid shack with the cute new attendant,
or maybe in the foremen's shack getting warm
while the rest of us freeze our butts off here in the hole down below,
you're The Man. And we know it's your way or the highway so please
give us another chance to earn our daily break and next time we promise,
we'll work the way you like it and be ready for concrete by four
but we hope you're in a better mood because yesterday
it was hell to please you.

Our foreman, we promise to work even harder if you'll accept that
once in a while mistakes happen. So forgive us for slacking off yesterday
and we'll forget the time you told us to frame in the third floor
when we were still on the second.

Also we'd really appreciate an advance on Friday's pay only
this time please don't tempt us by suggesting we buy you a beer
or two after work because we know you're the boss but so's the wife
and layoffs can happen at a minute's notice.
So thanks for understanding. We know you're cool and you've got
the power and whatever glory comes with this job,
at least for now. We know that. Also
that there's a meeting coming up and talk of organizing.
Amen.

First Woman

They huddle close
to each other, talking
shop, chanting confirmation
of every male rite.
Male-clad, afraid

as if I hide some terrible weapon,
as if we fight a war
only they can remember.

JOCKS

Baseballs, basketballs, golf balls and polo, volleyballs, soccer balls, tennis, lacrosse, cricket balls, pool, croquet and rugby. Badminton has no ball. Only a cock. Rhymes with jock.

Lately I've been reading between the lines. One sportscaster said to the coach who was given the game puck, *"Game puck" doesn't ring the same as "game ball,"* does it? Coach was silent.

The man beside me at the lacrosse game yells to his team, *Keep up your dicks!* I jerk back in alarm as he yells again, *Keep up your sticks!*

When women performed the rites, they called us witches and burned us. Now we worship the men—three strikes and they're out—with ten-million-dollar signing bonuses, pay money to watch them play with balls.

BREASTS

The people I work with
have flat chests.
No telltale bra lines, no straps,
nothing between them
and a plain white T-shirt
when the sweat sticks.

So today when I caught
a glimpse of myself
in a newly installed window,
reflection of a woman
with breasts
       two, not small, rather nice
       plainly female
I was shocked.

SPIKE LADY

They call me Spike Lady,
the one who wants to nail by hand
when she could have the nail gun any time,
the one that spits nails as fast as
you can pound its nose into the ground.

They boast the nail gun can shoot
a nail through a two-by-four in a split second,
through a man's skull
even quicker.

They call me Spike Lady,
the one who wants to nail by hand,
likes the cool steel of spikes
rolling through her fingers,
the fingerprint of her hammer
marking each piece well-joined.

They prefer the nailing gun, screw gun—
anything to drive those babies home
faster, harder.
Must be a gender thing.
We girls are so timid, so shy.

I pick up another handful of spikes
and raise my right arm, ready.

He Calls Me

After a conversation with a female firefighter

Because I don't carry a purse
or wear makeup

because I like sports
and am physically fit

because I wear a uniform
and the gods didn't make me pretty

because I wear boots
and am a firefighter, proud like him,

he calls me *Dyke Bitch Broad.*
I call him *Bill.*

THE DREAM

she who walks in deep water
she who bears a heavy weight
      who loses her footing, slips
           without air
           without breath

she who drowns

she who clings because the weight is known
because it is an old, old burden
because her arms have held its shape
for so long

because she always has
because she must

lets go

then she who gains wings
who is light
lifts

CAMP JOB: WELDER
for Marilyn

Sure, most jobs are OK but I remember one that wasn't, riding
the bus at 3 a.m. with a bunch of boilermakers trying to gross me
out, the only female welder, going into every gory detail of their sex
lives.

Either they never worked with a woman before or they just didn't
give a fiddler's fart but I memorized every one of their faces and
thought I'll know you tomorrow buddy so don't expect a cheery
Good Morning. They had no respect, those guys.

If I don't get respect, I wither on the vine. I need a warm place to
grow, you know? So it was nice on the next job where the guys were
decent, but the company was so badly organized, I'd start on one
job and five minutes later get moved to another then back to the
first. I was always asking, What am I doing now? and I guess I said
it a few times 'cause the guys started a song, Marilyn the Wonder
Welder Wonders What She's Welding. Even the foreman hummed it.

On Mother's Day, my day—I've got two kids, you know—I made
them promise not to sing it until midnight so they whistled it all
afternoon and at midnight burst into full chorus with harmony.
Good fun, you know?

At the tail end of another job a new welder came up to me—knew
me from union meetings—said, *Marilyn I can't believe you're really
doing this.* I said, Give your head a shake. On that job, a guy from
South America taught us all one step of the lambada every night.
When they laid us off we formed one big line and did the lambada.
Sure it was sexy, but it was fun. The new guy was shocked at me all
over. He had no sense of haha.

That guy was so far up the foreman's bum he couldn't see the light of day, said to my friend Ben that having women on the job was kind of novel. Ben hit the roof, told him he'd worked with two women welders and both of us pulled our weight and gave him a hand when he needed it. Told him women aren't here for his entertainment, aren't novel. We're welders.

A guy like Ben makes you feel good, eh? Last year when I was teaching, one student called the Native guy Chief, and I said, In this course we call people by their first name. If you don't know his first name you can call him Brother.

They can call me Sister. That's when it feels good, like I belong, all of us flourishing on one big vine.

WCB

No woman shall have to endure a single sexist statement or act.
Exposure causes undue stress and hardship. Perpetrators will
be dealt with immediately.
       —Regulation 1:01, Newest Century's Workers'
              Compensation Standards

Flash! The Workers' Compensation Board
has just revealed the discovery
of a virulent new breed of
occupational disease now spreading
with virus-like intensity.

Defined as "arrogant, insensitive,
harassing behaviour toward women,"
the disease has now been listed as
Regulation Number 1 and the WCB declares
Zero Tolerance.

Today rumours spread that a second disease
closely affiliated to the first has been
uncovered. It is said to be associated with race.

The virus was denounced by a whistle-blower
whose revolutionary work has been awarded
a Purple Heart for Service to Humanity
and Genius in Recognition of the Obvious.
Scientists at the Board were quoted as saying,
"We don't know how we missed it."

The Board announces that henceforth
demeaning and sexist and racist statements
will be treated in Category 99
of Useless Occupational Traditions.

The first case was discovered within minutes
and the perpetrator dealt with before lunch.
Lawyers and judges have been alerted
that this behaviour is epidemic
and to be on the alert. Courts are poised
for a landslide number of detentions.

Only the supreme penalty will be inflicted,
to whit, all sufferers will be immediately
put out of their misery with injections of
reality. Families may report to the Board
to claim the final remains of sexist, racist fantasies.

"Girl" on the Crew

The boys flap heavy leather aprons at me
like housewives scaring crows
from the clean back wash.
   Some aprons. Some wash.

They think if the leather is tough enough,
if the hammer handle piercing it is long enough,
I will be overcome with primordial dread
or longing.

They chant construction curses at me:
   Lay 'er down! Erect those studs!
and are alarmed when I learn the words.

They build finely tuned traps, give orders I cannot fill,
then puzzle when a few of their own
give me passwords.

I learn the signs of entry,
dropping my hammer into its familiar mouth
as my apron whispers *O-o-o-h Welcome!*

I bite off nails with my teeth,
shorten boards with a wave of my hand,
pierce them through the dark brown love knots.
The boys gasp.

I point my finger and corner posts spring into place,
shivering themselves into fertile earth at my command.
The surveyors have never seen such accuracy.

I squat and the flood of my urine digs
whole drainage systems in an instant.
The boys park their backhoes, call their friends
to come see for themselves or they'd never believe it.

The hairs of my head turn to steel and join boards
tongue-in-groove
like lovers along dark lanes.
Drywall is rustling under cover
eager to slip over the studs at my desire.

When I tire, my breasts grow two cherry trees
that offer me shade, cool juices,
while the others suck bitter beans.

At the end of the day the boys are exhausted
from watching.
They fall at my feet and beg for a body like mine.
I'm too busy dancing to notice.

Summer Rites

All right you guys, you win!
Here's one more
hell of a hot day
and you with your bare chests
have asked once too often
that stunningly witty question,
When will you *take off* your *T-shirt, Kate?*

So here I go! Open your eyes and look!
No T-shirt now, just me
and my skin feels great
in the cool tingle of breeze
at last drying sweat.
Already I feel brown all over.
Why haven't I done this
                              sooner?

What?
It embarrasses you to see
my biceps flash
when I swing this hammer?
You never knew it was muscle
                              beneath all these curves?

You want what?
No brother.
When the shirt comes off
                              it's off.
You'll simply have
to lower your eyes
when the woman walks by.

Sacrament: Building the House on 42nd Avenue

Bending—half priest, half peasant—
she serves her creation
as shadows of rafter throw
blueprints over her floor.
In this shelter she worships,
watches it
rise, iridescent with lightness
each day further above her,
bones rising, flesh
from her flesh,
its creaking breath of two-by-fours
awakened
by the kiss of her hammer.

CONTRADICTIONS

Going back to work this time
I'd almost forgotten how easily
some men fall in love
with a woman who bridges the gap,
who teases their manhood
at its root, at work,
who shakes it a little
with that style of feminine
that swings a mean hammer.

I'd almost forgotten
the moment of light in their eyes
when they hear themselves say,
I liked working with you today.
And the confusion
later
when they stumble
over this new knowledge.

I'd almost forgotten the time
when I complained my hands
were like sandpaper
and Charlie laughed.
You're supposed to say
they're getting nicely into shape!
Or the time he moved a wall
three-quarters of an inch
with two spikes and a 28-ounce hammer and said,
Carpenters are nice people because
the material we work with
is so forgiving.

I had almost forgotten the contradictions,
so onion sweet
they make my eyes water.

BROTHERS

for Roger

We have worked together
eight hours every day,
five days every week,
four weeks every month
for three months now.
Closer than a marriage
in the intensity of our days,
the joy in our joint production.

We have fought for each other
and refused to be separated
by other carpenters
or a foreman's whim,
and yesterday they said
next week there will be layoffs.

When tears sprang to my eyes
you said, *Don't get excited.*
You've said it many times.
It's our joke of the past three months
and now I understand
that *excited* means *emotional.*
I'm not allowed to care on this job
yet you're grateful I speak the unspoken,
cry tears for us all.

GREAT MOMENTS IN CONSTRUCTION

1. The Carpenter
In memory of Jacqueline Frewin

This too is camaraderie
to sit at midnight
with another woman carpenter.

By noon we'd kicked the drywallers off the job
for gross incompetence
and now we've finished their work
in time for tomorrow's deadline.

We sit, exhausted by a sixteen-hour day,
drinking peppermint tea and laughing
over how we'd have acted
if *we'd* been stoned on this job.

I would've measured the space
between nails, you say
and we giggle
                    giddy with fatigue

then sit silent in the beam of a trouble light,
admiring our work,
proud of what we've done,
proud
            we've done it together.

2. The Plumber

The plumber gives excellent service.
We're all impressed by how early he gets to work,
how late he stays. We tell him to ease off
but he insists he doesn't mind working Saturday—again.

Later we find the note with flowers
for the nanny in the basement suite
signed *Love, The Plumber.*

3. The Concrete Finisher

The pit floor in the elevator shaft
on 14th Avenue is filling with water.
Nobody knows what to do
but there've been no lack of suggestions.
Maybe it's the joins, someone says.
Finish the drain tile first, adds another.

We who built it—
two carpenters and a concrete finisher—
stand close, our arms swung vine-like
around fragrant lumber, hanging
over the black, mouldy smell
of elevator turned sump.

Vern, the concrete finisher,
pokes with a stick and we all stare dumbly
at the shocking levels of water revealed
by the wet wood, luminous
in the near dark.

Vern drops his head as if to listen
to the tinkle of water.
I think, he says
in an accent thick with the florals
of the Caribbean,
*You can't do a damn thing 'til you figure out
where this water coming from.*
And we hang like three flowers—
two pinks and a chocolate brown—
waiting for the answer to rise up
from the five o'clock depths of a Friday afternoon
at the elevator shaft.

4. The Salesman

The salesman from the window company
is short
      and round.
His name is Bill and he mops his forehead
frequently,
sees nothing wrong with plastic arches
in a solid wood door
but is happy to discuss it
      at length.

Bill talks
      a lot.
Sometimes we women keep working—
carpenter, contractor, apprentice—
while Bill tells about cheap drinks
in Blaine. One day he comes right out
and asks the contractor to go
for a beer with him.
She's in a ditch at the time
laying drain tile, wading
         in mud.

Bill arrives one day waving a sheet
of paper, hot off the library's copy machine.
I looked up your company name,
ZENOBIA, he says
and shows the picture of an Amazon queen
looking so like the woman in front of him
      she might have been her mother.

He reads bits of the story aloud
and we all stop work to listen, hear his voice
rise in alarm when it comes to the part
where Zenobia kills off her husband.

The contractor looks over Bill's shoulder.
Yes, she says. *That was before divorce,*
and goes back
    to her drain tile.

5. The Drywaller

The drywaller is a Buddhist.
When the foreman calls him for work
he can't come to the phone because
      he's chanting.
The drywaller is working on
his spiritual development
on levels far different from the daily ones
of cut and lift and nail
that he practises
all day
      every week
            all year.

The drywaller announces that he marches
to a different drummer.
Which explains, perhaps,
the three-hour lunches
from which he returns—sort of—
in a way suggestive of
      something—beer perhaps—
the work of his body opposed
to the work of his soul.

CRUCIFIED

for Bishop Remi de Roo

You say if Jesus returned
we would know him
by his hands.

You could say that about
any carpenter,
the seams and calluses
of our palms marking us

permanently
as people of the outdoors
stroking rough wood
every day in every weather.

A simple religion of labour,
our crucifixion would be
      to make us stop,
our resurrection
      the chance to work again.

GENERAL STRIKE, 1987
for Ray Heaton

See this sign? *In Protest* it says but it says more, things you won't see
printed here no matter how hard you strain those eyes. It says I'm
fed up with all this farting around. I can't talk pretty like some but
I know I vote for every damned thing in my union. Now tell me the
last time the boss asked my opinion on the foreman's salary or how
fast the green chain moves, though nobody knows better than me
what could make this place hum for the better of us all.

I give 'em my blood and my muscle for eight hours every day and
still they say "when" I work and "if" and "when" I take a break and
"if" and whether they'll give me earmuffs for the job or if I got to
buy my own, though without 'em you go deaf real fast and some
days it's half an hour overtime no extra pay 'cause the boss has a
rush on, no matter that I'm the one got to pick up the kid 'cause the
wife works afternoons.

So when they said I have too much power I damn split a gut
laughing 'til they told me I didn't have a job no more. If this is too
much power then what do I make of Timothy Eaton or Conrad
Black who don't seem too worried about the next mortgage
payment or if they can send their kid to a better school 'cause
teacher says she's bright.

Me and the people like me, we built this province board by board
and we built it good and if this government says I'm a traitor
for asking for a steady job or the right to question what they do
to make my work life worse, then I'm on the march. Do you see
this sign? It says I'm fed up with all this farting around.

Union Love Poem: For Local 452/1995

We meet in small backrooms and union halls,
me the only woman with these plain brown men.
We argue for hours over strategy, laughing
when things threaten to become personal, dig in
for another round. We are planning our future.

Tonight John leans forward, red plaid jacket brushing mine,
and points to the sawdust on my knees.
Bet you put that there on purpose.
I smile. He knows I spent this day renovating.
Eau de sawdust, Bill whispers from the other side.

When the meeting adjourns we push back our chairs,
trade jokes and news.
First, *Are you working?* Then, *Where?*
It's banter, but underneath it is the bedrock certainty
that these men, carpenters all, would be pillars to hold to
should any of us fall on a job, in a strike, on a picket line.
And here tonight in this roomful of brothers
I know the meaning of *camaraderie.*

UNION WELDERS: OVERTIME
for Sandy Shreve

My brothers are building a dome
of crazed bars jutting stiff into Expo air.

Stopped at the streetlight in darkness
I look up to watch them
hundreds of feet off the ground,
magnificently poised up where the air is clear.
They are stars to me, shooting novas
as they strike arcs, set their welding rods
and build.

Those aren't welders, my son explains
from the passenger seat beside me.
He is sixteen and wise.
Those are lights set to flash.
Construction is finished, done.

And suddenly this dome is joyless to me.
I see builders no more, just the built,
ugly attempt to mimic heaven.
When the light turns green, I hit the gas too hard.
The car jerks forward. We move on.

CARPENTER

everyone has scars…
—Michael Ondaatje, "Signature"

This is who I am,
this is what I do,
these are the scars I bear:

thick fingers of muscle, scar tissue
over old cuts from the utility knife,
chisels that missed, nails that didn't,
one finger gimped by a hammer that fell
too soon, fingernails that
out of politeness
should never be outlined again in red,
hands that in your wildest imaginings
you couldn't call soft.

Here's a back that aches regardless
of stretches each morning,
and a steady cough
from my allergy to wood dust.

I also show a tendency to talk
to my wood.
Some call it madness, others
nod. They've seen it before
in a pride that says, *I built that,*
and a love a mile wide
for my fellow carpenters because
I know their secrets,
our shared passion for wood
no matter what.

WORLD CUP SOCCER

This soaring game in which every player
wears concentration like a skin,
each body like Nureyev's flying
higher than the next man's
toward that desperately sought-after
firefly, the soccer ball.

France vs. Norway, Brazil vs. Spain,
their bodies speak the familiar language
of men in action—fierce competition
for a ball, a symbol in this head-knocking race
for mastery. And at the end, a grudging respect
for the muscle of it, the head-cracking, joint-knocking,
ball-kicking explosion of strength and skill and even luck
they will celebrate later.

But for now, it's the pure pleasure of the doing
in a race for the best, and men who finally,
in this celebration of the body,
can afford to embrace and cry
at last.

Thanks for the Load

Crunched on, crammed into man-sized
steel-toed boots, there's no arch support
for my woman's feet. Toes rub raw
and when the boots are new, heels too.
I haul my one-hundred-fifty pounds
plus two-by-fours, plywood, boxes of nails,
up ladders, across joists, through mud
to the place they're needed and feet
get me there, kick walls into place,
loosen stubborn stakes, test nails.
How many roots and steel rods have I tripped over?
How many country roads run?
I massage my arms, stretch my back
and never think to give a small word of thanks
to my feet.

WHY STAY, CARPENTER?
for Terence Young, who asked

This hand with the hammer,
this arm with its silky sheen of sweat
overlaid with the black lace of dust,
surely this limb, this trunk of flesh and muscle
anchors me, is proof that I belong, tells me at last
I am here, I can stay.

TEN

I was all cheeky and bone and ready to fight
so even if the boys made me go last,
I crossed narrow planks over treacherous
sewage lines and ditches into half-built houses
with the rest of them.

I was glorious until the day I rushed
to play soccer with my brothers and
my father, who reached out his hand to
push me gently in the chest.
Boys only, he said. *Go home.*
And shoved my skinny girl's body away from me.

But today he needs a new wall in his house
and all morning my father and I move
from lumber yard to tile store
where I pass the tests, know
which way a door is hung and how to carry drywall.
Dad asks, *Can I help?*
and my forty-year-old body
steps into the game, at last.

Jesus' Younger Sister

She hung around her father, this one, loved
the low dusky shed where he planed curls
off sweet-smelling cedar.

A curious child, not sent to school,
somehow she learned in the glow
of late afternoons when her father, resting,
answered her endless questions. Watching him,
she learned by mime the rhythms of his trade.

Often her mother found the child in the work shed,
running her hands over fine ribs, reading
the messages left by the wood plane's passage.
Chased back to the kitchen over and over
the girl returned 'til finally
she was left in peace with her father.

He had given up trying to teach his son.
The boy couldn't settle, wanted to be out all day,
talking in the temple instead of learning his trade.
The father accepted his daughter instead, showed her
how the tools could work, let her hold
the ends of fine woods he carved
into shelves and furniture, the odd cross.

The first time the girl picked up a chisel
and touched it to wood, wood responded
like flesh to her fingers.

More patient than her brother, she carved
crown flower and alyssum, almond and amaranth,
hedgehog, deer, red fox and squirrels,
let the dumb wood speak.
Neighbours gathered to watch.
She performs miracles with wood, they said,
brings dead animals to life,
makes wooden flowers bloom.

Now sometimes you see her alone in her shop
in cedar-scented air, sharpening her tools or resting,
studying her folded hands, callused and cut,
the scars on her palms.

GOLD MINING CAMP: NORTHERN BRITISH COLUMBIA

A ragged field, ten tents, a cookshack, muddy lake
and forty miners, carpenters—all men and me

under the crackle and green of northern lights, my life
as a carpenter shaken

to a shape that claims me, a flicker of confidence
as I move through a sheen of mountain air.

The other carpenters, all Native, eye me, me them,
then nod over something understood.

My shoulders settle easy into a carpenter's harness.
All those years of trying to belong, building

roads, bridges, houses, all that trying to rise up and over—
tower, bean stalk, vines—not knowing that all along

I was my own golden princess.
And now I find in the most unlikely spot

(it was so simple and I'd thought it would be hard)
no fairy tale but a nod, alchemy of mud and green yielding gold.

THESE HIPS

Some hips are made for bearing
children, built like stools
square and easy, right
for the passage of birth.

Others are built like mine.
A child's head might never pass
but load me up with two-by-fours
and watch me
bear.

When the men carry sacks of concrete
they hold them high, like boys.
I bear mine low, like a girl
on small, strong hips
built for the birth
of buildings.

WHERE FROM? WHERE TO?

STEP SON

for Kevin Steeves

For someone who never gave birth
I'm not doing too bad,
sitting in this high school auditorium just like
a real parent,
trying not to be too obvious when I wave back at
the sort-of-subtle flourishes of the first clarinet.

Positively dashing, this child not-of-my-body,
born of seven years of my care.
My heart dances with gratitude,
me who was always too impatient
to wait for a baby to grow, now blessed
with a fifteen-year-old man who bends
from six feet of solicitude and honours me
with the question asked only of friends,
How's it goin', dude?

AMELIA GWENDOLYN, 1886–1982

Some of my ancestors were women,
lived alongside their men
      unnoticed
except when married,
            commended
for invisibility.

Some of my ancestors
rocked the boat
along with the cradle and sang
warrior songs
      with lust in their eyes
caught food and killed it and ate
and thanked the goddess.
           Carried on.

Bore babies, some of my ancestors did,
raised bees, mowed hay
and all along they were heras
that nobody noticed,
          forgotten,
except for the odd
line in Amelia's Bible, the odd
word like a seed
just waiting
      for water.

STRONG ARMS, STRONG HEART: 1925
for my grandmother, Sarah Baker Shepherdson

Four children I have
and a farm. No man.

A yard full of dust
a heart full of wheat

and a Bible I wear
like a breastplate of salvation.

At twenty I came from Dublin
with a dowry of quilts and lace,
a history of selling fine hats.

The house was as he said,
still creaking fresh and smelling of honey
in the middle of a Prairie sea,
no woman for miles.

Rich in children, I built a world
out of soap and water, ashes and lye
my own strong arms, strong heart.

When the man died, I worked harder.
Sent the boys to school. The girls
carried milk, piled hay, ran horses,
cooked for the hired men at harvest.

When I die, the boys will take the farm.
The girls will marry. It is God's will, it is
what I have lived for.

Four children I have
and a farm. No man.

A yard full of dust
a heart full of wheat

and a Bible I wear
like a breastplate of salvation.

AUNTIE

for Kathleen Coates and Kelly Pryde

In dreams I draw my finger over your dusty welding rods
forbidden since the war when they said
married women can't do men's work anymore,
should be home minding babies, sewing smocks for new citizens.
A woman's place, you always said, is where she wants to be.

That was the war we all lost, that time.

This Aching

My muscles grow taut from physical work
and what shall I do with this clenching?

I lay my hurting body, an offering
on the masseuse's table.
Her hands and shoulders, strong like mine, work
to loosen knots of muscle.

But after, I wonder—where does the pain go?
Does it seep from my skin into hers?
What aching of mine does she carry home at night?
Who takes her tired shoulders after a day of blessing
the rest of us, and gives her ease?

BUSH PILOT: 1

In memory of Theresa Bond

Remember how they said
women can't fly this plane
      (crude jokes about Beavers)
and I told you the secret, that
it doesn't take a man
to push a button marked Power!

But they kept talking and after a while
I started to wonder (the doubt like rust)
maybe I *couldn't* fly.

That time I helped John load the plane,
he said slow down but I loaded double I was
going to show them, until my left arm slipped
and the bucket pulled my arm down hard
so I hit my jaw on the step.

I said nothing, kept loading.
John flew away and still I said nothing
for one more month. The jaw was broken.

What does it take?

BUSH PILOT: 2

Defying the evidence of their own eyes
they lied, insisted women—especially
small women like me—can't fly.

But I kept flying, kept carrying
people, freight, balancing barrels
of oil and machinery
over mountains,
ill will trailing like exhaust.
The plane was shrouded with it.

They said one woman
can't.   I didn't know
I too   was caught

until that day on Dease Lake—
five passengers and the water
like a mirror, so calm
even the lake was distorted
so I trusted the surface too late,
looked right through it,
pushing the nose down
to kiss my plane's reflection
under water. Too late. Another
lie.

BUSH PILOT: 3

Don't kid yourself
I am
shattered glass
I am
putting the pieces back together
the accident was
my fault
I am responsible   the water was glass
I could only see my reflection
they said I couldn't   but
a pilot is   of course   I take
full responsibility

apart from my jaw outside and hurt
on the inside
there were no other injuries
to me
but I am responsible
for the others

I thought I would go crazy

women as far away as Telegraph Creek
write
We don't know what to say but
we love you

when we hit I was thrown out
through the space where the windshield
used to be
and as soon as I came to
under water
I knew
I was the only one alive and I thought
I only have to take

a mouthful   one
deep breath
and it will all be over but
I didn't
I kept going under

I can't swim you know but
somehow I came up
for the rescue

don't laugh but
all my life I've tested myself
asked, *what's the worst that could happen?*
and the worst was that I would crash
and kill somebody and me
alive

I ask myself   *why am I alive?*

that night another pilot visited me
in the clinic
only small talk but
he'll never know how much it meant

he looked me straight in the eye, said,
you'd do the same for me

I am a piece of glass
shattered and now
I have to put together the pieces
and I   will
I will put together   everything
but

I could have just died

the day after the crash
they wired shut my jaw
and after two weeks I wanted to scream,
took the pliers and pulled out the strands
that were muzzling me

it's the women mostly
they keep me from going crazy
one woman widowed twice
came to my house and said
*I forgive you
and when you forgive yourself
you will be whole*

the women are the strongest
they are a ray of light and
don't kid yourself

I will
put together
all
the pieces.

BUSH PILOT: 4

Dear Theresa,
You mourned and were crazy, especially when your husband died within months of the crash. But you found a new man (or he found you), someone who cheered for your side for a change, and you began again, putting it all together.

The neighbours sniffed and disapproved and wouldn't speak to That Man in your house but he made you laugh and you started eating again. (*She even got tits,* he told me.) When I saw the pictures of you one year later I didn't recognize you, laughing and happy.

They promised the two of you a job together training staff for a Western-style hotel in China. *My energy, her brains,* he said. *We needed three months to clear up loose ends, time to get married, then to China for two years.*

All the pieces, together again.

BUSH PILOT: 5

Sister, it makes me grieve, how
the newspapers gave the barest account.
They always treated you barely.
But they had time to say,
The same woman pilot of the plane that crashed,
killing five. They listed all your previous accidents,
your mistakes meant to explain everything.

They got you in the end. Dead
by some other pilot's hand.
They didn't specify, *Male pilot makes error, kills self*
and two others, a woman and a five-year-old child.

They didn't list his previous accidents,
let the man rest in peace,
something they don't allow you
lest some other woman take up the challenge,
press the right buttons
without a single thing between her legs
except the ordinary
courage, every woman's

                          power.

THE TASTE OF PINK

Last month with hundreds of men in one room
I hardly noticed the tightness of their flat hard chests
muscled smooth beneath plaid shirts,
bass voices whose rumble I now accept
as normal.

So sitting with these women I'm culture shocked
amid a hundred pairs of breasts
roiling round and warm over these flat hard eyes.
I'm dazzled by cotton and silk cascading off
round hills of hips, colours so strong they pulse
a treble of purple and red
and my tongue feels thick with the taste of pink.

CRONES

All the old women are smiling.
It's a small fixed smile.

When they laugh
it's the cough of the eagle,

a hum that grows to a sound like thunder,
a pick, pick, picking.

All the old women are digging.
Urgent now. At last

their voices ring out, released.
They are digging through the rock of centuries.

I lean forward, eager to see what they find.

CREATION

It's sure as stone, they say: we women
have a biological urge to produce only babies.

But what choice have we had,
pressed to create cakes, cookies, children?

For centuries we dozed through the fairy tales, waiting.
But lately bells are ringing, there are cracks

in the paving stones of tradition through which
the wild weeds among us have forced ourselves.

We women rustle, restless with dreams of becoming
our own knights valiant, freeing ourselves and each other

from the bonds of sleep and forgetting, stone
becoming sculpture, each of us—artist.

WOMAN WHO KNOWS WOOD

A History of My Meetings with Emily Carr

1. National Gallery, Ottawa

In these early paintings, Emily,
I was happy enough. You had become
a carver of space and colour modelled
after the poles you loved but now
as I turn to the large wall, suddenly this.
Shocked at the licentiousness of greens,
I grow flustered, forget to look for a title.
Order slips while Eros grows up my legs
and my nipples harden
under the promise of bark.

Surely this picture should be hidden by draperies?
Emily, such a tree from you, sixty years old
and eccentric as all get-out,
promenading with your monkey and dogs
down Government Street.
A Victorian woman, you, and yet
these paintings show no shame, as if
you wouldn't even shriek when another pole—
huge, dark, male—entered your canvas,
straining to meet with the sky.

I am afraid to meet the eyes of other tourists,
afraid they will see the lust carved here.
I fall into a chair for relief. Someone
give me a merely obsessive Michael Snow!

Emily, you! Old and fat and daring to flaunt
such spirit! Is this why Lawren Harris
encouraged you from a distance?
Surely he licked his lips when another of your
cedar-heavy boxes arrived, breathing musk and dark,
while his own canvases lay frozen in ice.

2. British Columbia Forest

Emily, I could taste you,
the salad of your palette,
bitter chocolate of tree trunks
and totem poles climbing into skies drenched
with green and blue and light.

And down below,
when green ran like smoke through the forest,
ripe with the smell of feasts coming,
what did you do then, hungry,
on your little camp stool, in your caravan
with only the poles and the trees and the paint?

3. *Tree*

Stand back! This tree is going places!
It's a thunder of branches,
a wilderness of wind,
a highwayman riding, riding
through a stormy night, a teamster's whip
as tree boughs whistle and lock
to the sharp brown shouts of cedar and pine.

And here's the small green at the heart of things.

Notice how this tree doesn't fall but
lays itself down, gives itself
when no one is looking,
for love, for a wild desire.

Night blinks wide in shock.
Moon blanches. Sky is a memory.
What is real is this—love unleashed,
an epic of tree trunk and limbs.

So ride on, ride on. Now we know
woodsmen only carry axes
to cut themselves free. Ride on!

4. *Loggers' Culls*

She paints
another landscape wiped bare
by careless human hands—
here it's loggers' culls,
there, a city.

Something has died.

Only the clouds are alive,
one stand of forest,
and there, to the left,
a crystal ball of ghosts.

The sky knows. It ties itself
into a tight blue knot.
Whirlwind with no way out,
it circles, keening.
At its centre shines
a deep blue eye.

5. *Wood Interior*, 1909

There it is, earlier still.
Such a naive picture, with all the parts
we are supposed to recognize
as bark, leaves, branches, green in its place.
You felt it like that then.

But even this early your spirit stares
and sees what is between the trees,
joining them. It is a space
any carpenter would understand.
It is the reason we build things.
Looks like air to some,
fresh breeze, a touch of chill or fog.
It is the spirit of the tree.

Now I know who you are.
Another woman who knows wood.

ACKNOWLEDGEMENTS

With thanks to the publications and editors who have previously published poems in this collection: *Antigonish Review, Canadian Dimension, Contemporary Verse 2, Don't Quit Yr Day-Job, Fireweed, Labor: Studies in Working-Class History of the Americas, Malahat Review, Ms.* magazine, *Our Times, PRISM International, Room* magazine, *This* magazine, *Tradeswomen,* and the United Steelworkers Métallos participants' education manual *(Stewards in Action 1).* Also the anthologies *111 West Coast Literary Portraits* (Mother Tongue Press), *East of Main* (Pulp Press), *More Than Our Jobs* (Pulp Press), *Paperwork* (Harbour Publishing) and *If I Had a Hammer* (Papier-Maché Press). The poem *"Loggers' Culls"* won first prize in the Saving Wildwood Poetry Contest in Nanaimo, BC, in 2001 and was published in the chapbook *Saving Trees, Saving Wildwood.*

Deepest thanks to my family and all the community of poets and writers who keep me going, to Patricia Young for fresh eyes, to Vici Johnstone, publisher extraordinaire, and to the wonderful crew at Caitlin Press— Andrea Routley, Benjamin Dunfield and Kathleen Fraser—and, always, to John Steeves for unwavering support.

Photo: Barry Peterson

Starting in the 1970s, Kate Braid worked for fifteen years as a construction labourer, apprentice and journey carpenter doing union and non-union work as well as running her own small renovations company. She has since written eleven books of poetry and non-fiction, most recently *Journeywoman: Swinging a Hammer in a Man's World*, a memoir about her years in the trade.

Caitlin Press Inc.
8100 Alderwood Road,
Halfmoon Bay, BC V0N 1Y1
www.caitlin-press.com

Text design by Benjamin Dunfield
Editor: Patricia Young
Cover Design: Vici Johnstone
Printed in Canada

Caitlin Press Inc. acknowledges financial support from the Government of Canada and
the Canada Council for the Arts, and from the Province of British Columbia through
the British Columbia Arts Council and the Book Publisher's Tax Credit.

Library and Archives Canada Cataloguing in Publication

Braid, Kate, 1947-
[Poems. Selections]
    Rough ground revisited / Kate Braid.

Rough Ground Revisited includes some poems previously included in
    Covering Rough Ground, published in 1991, as well as some new
    poems.
ISBN 978-1-927575-93-2 (paperback)

    I. Title.

PS8553.R2585R68 2015   C811'.54   C2015-904045-0

This book is set in Arno Pro. Designed by Robert Slimbach, Arno was crafted in the tradition of early Venetian and Aldine book types. Named after the river that runs through Florence, the center of the Italian Renaissance, Arno draws on the warmth and readability of early humanist types of the 15th and 16th centuries. The text was typeset by Benjamin Dunfield.
Caitlin Press, Fall 2015.
ΕΟ